MW00443088

FROM SURVIVING TO VIBING

FILLING IN THE GAPS

Tips and tricks for tweens, teens, and young adults (and their parents)

BY CARRON MONTGOMERY, MSCP, LPC, RPT
CAROLINE DANDA, PHD, LP

ILLUSTRATIONS BY DAVID GENTILE • GRAPHICS BY MIRANDA LUCAS
GRAPHIC CONTRIBUTORS: CORIE ENGLISH AND SARAH GOLDER

DONNELLY-KILROY PUBLICATIONS

From Surviving to Vibing: Filling in the Gaps

Part of The Invisible Riptide series

Dedicated to our inspiring clients, who continue to persevere despite many challenges. You are showing the world that MENTAL HEALTH matters. We learn so much from you! Your voices are important and deserve to be heard. Thank you to our families, friends, and our own personal villages who allowed us the space and support to write this book.

We are so grateful for the support and encouragement of our families, grandparents, aunts, and uncles. This book is truly a product of community effort and the wisdom of multiple generations. We learned that everything is more fun together and even feels like less work. We hope you enjoy reading this book as much as we appreciate being part of this journey with you.

INTRODUCTION.

Hi! Thanks for picking up this book. The tsunami of events and emotions associated with the Coronavirus pandemic, combined with social and political unrest in the world today exaggerated an already complex world. It's not easy to make sense of the constant stream of information, messages, and media. Furthermore, many people simply don't have access to a therapist or other resources to help make sense of what is happening in their mind, body, and world. This book is designed to fill that gap.

You need to know YOU ARE NOT ALONE. We are on this journey together, and we will make our way through it together. This book provides some operating instructions to gain an awareness of how your brain and body work together, so you are more equipped to navigate a world full of challenging situations, pandemic or not.

If your parents pick up this book (and we hope they do), they will likely gain greater insight into your world and be inspired by your perseverance and acceptance of mental health. Although adults may remember being insecure and vulnerable at your age, it's almost impossible to grasp how much the pandemic and social media magnified these issues. Filling in the gaps across generations creates a shared, more accurate understanding that promotes connection and discussion so you can use your voice to advocate and work together.

HELLO PANDEMIC WORLD.

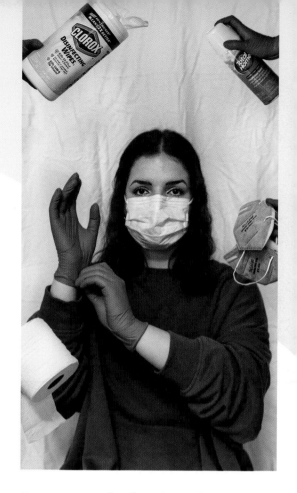

The world changed dramatically with the abrupt onset of Coronavirus. Social media and news feeds provide a constant barrage of unsettling, ever-changing news that emphasizes a slew of unknowns in a nonstop feedback loop of worrisome topics. Home lives changed dramatically, at least for a time, as many youth became home-schoolers and parents became work-from-home-ers, while simultaneously trying to support their children's schooling at home. The world experienced one disappointing cancellation after another. Some parents lost their jobs and felt the daily stress of trying to make ends meet. Many didn't and still haven't seen grandparents and relatives for a long time. You likely lost or know someone who lost a loved one to Coronavirus. It's layer upon layer of grief and disappointment.

Fun parts of school, such as hanging out with friends and free periods, were the first to go and are still not the same. Laughing with peers and having freedom helps make hard work more bearable and creates more incentive to go to school. With the loss of fun, resuming school was too much, too soon, too fast. As if the changes in school weren't enough, the controversy surrounding politics, masking, vaccinations, and racism was yet another layer that added to emotional distress.

Some describe the ongoing disruption, dysregulation, and uncertainty associated with the Coronavirus pandemic as traumatic. Trauma arises from experiences of heightened fear and anxiety and often has a cumulative effect. Each person perceives and stores what is traumatic differently. These factors associated with the pandemic can contribute to a traumatic or heightened stress response.

- Ongoing uncertainty and frequently changing information

- Fear of contracting or spreading Coronavirus

- Being isolated and unable to participate in typical activities

- Having or knowing someone who contracted the virus and became sick or died

- Mourning the loss of loved ones, as well as the loss of many of our usual routines, activities, and traditions

"Everyone was hanging on by a thread. You could feel the dread coming off of people, even professors — although that was more like a short fuse. I could feel it all around me. I've never experienced anything like that before."

–Freshman in college

• • •

Sometimes, it can feel impossible to identify and keep up with all the changes happening, not only in the outside world, but also in your inner world. Let's face it. In the midst of all this uncertainty, there has been very little clear communication, and some changes do not seem to make sense. Even though we are not quite as holed up and isolated in our homes, many report still feeling lonely, even being surrounded by peers. It's easier to accept loneliness when you are truly alone, than when you "should" feel better being around others.

If you don't know the "why" or understand something, your brain's first instinct is to fill in the gaps with the WORST-CASE scenario. Anxiety loves to attach to anything that is uncertain, unpredictable, or unknown — all consistent elements in this pandemic. It's no surprise that anxiety has skyrocketed in recent years. The reality is that the mental health ramifications will likely last much longer than the physical threat of the virus. We now know that it is important not only to have physical safety, but also to have **emotional safety** — the ability to recognize, experience, and express emotions.

Although many negatives surfaced, there were also some unexpected positives, courtesy of the pandemic.

- Increased focus on mental health
- Understanding that it's OK to not be OK
- Recognizing thoughts and feelings impact our emotional AND physical health
- Extra time with family and a temporary decrease in nonstop activities

Unfortunately, there is still a major gap in the depth of knowledge about mental health, especially across generations. More work needs to be done to change the way society looks at and supports mental health.

Hello thoughts!

In our practice, we see firsthand the ongoing negative effects of the pandemic. Here are examples of what we hear repeatedly in our offices. You may recognize some of these.

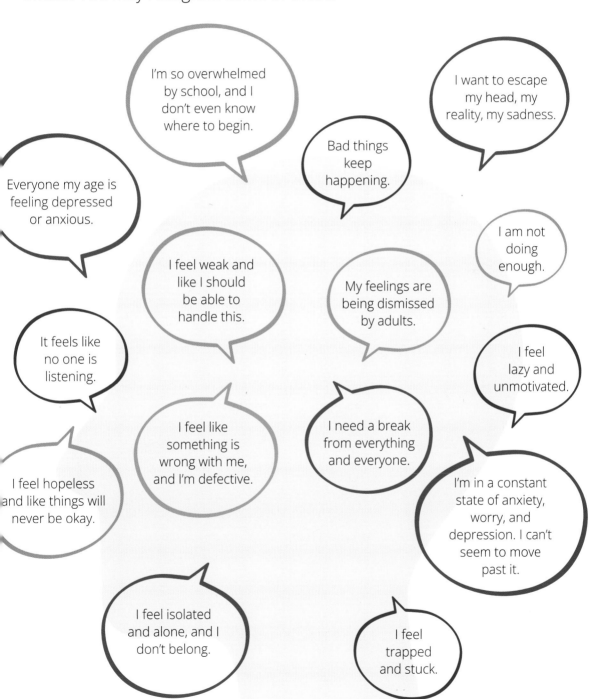

Spending endless amounts of time alone and "attending" school from your beds started a process that allowed more and more negative and unhelpful thoughts to pop up. Often, you start with one negative thought, and then other negative thoughts join, creating a downward spiral of doom and gloom. This spiral often happens at night when the busyness of the day is done.

Your brain's default becomes viewing the world through a negative lens. This can make it almost impossible to see that anything is going well. As people continue to feel raw, they are more vulnerable to becoming attached to negative thoughts that are harmful to their growing sense of self.

Learning to be alone with your thoughts without judgment is a skill that most never learn. Thoughts come from experiences you have, what you believe about yourself, what you hear from other people, and what you feel. Simply put, thoughts are messages and information to be evaluated. Once you become more aware of your thoughts, you can decide whether the thoughts are helpful and worth keeping or unhelpful and worth discarding.

● ● ●

HELLO EMOTIONS!

lazy
unsafe
hopeless relieved
anxious sad lonely
stupid frustrated
bored confused

As mental health clinicians, we watched people of all ages unravel in our offices. They were feeling overwhelmed, helpless, lonely, and frozen. It continues today. With uncertainty and change, it's natural to be confused and stuck, trapped in a quagmire of emotions. Feeling anxious, depressed, and stuck is not something new. The vast majority of people experience such feelings from time to time. Feeling stuck is a signal that you haven't stopped long enough to recognize your feelings, truly feel them, or express them.

If you don't understand what you're feeling or the purpose of feelings, you are more likely to feel overwhelmed and stuck. In fact, you may feel frustrated or guilty for feeling anxious or depressed, or that you should just snap out of it. These feelings-on-top-of-feelings intensify the negativity and cloud your thinking. In reality, your initial emotional reaction is appropriate. Your feelings are there to guide you.

Of course you might feel disappointed or discouraged if you weren't included in an activity. You might be frustrated if you don't do as well as expected. Sometimes situations do suck, and that's OK. Be compassionate toward yourself. Once you acknowledge and validate your feeling, you can figure out what to do with it, if anything. Choose to do something that helps you move through the feeling. Connect with a friend. Journal. Reach out to someone. Ask for help with studying. Make plans to go out another night. Craft. Exercise. Bake. Play a board game. Organize your closet. Curl up with a good book. Feelings are feelings. Validate them. Allow them to be. Move on.

So how can I figure out my feelings? Slow down, pause, and ask yourself — what am I feeling? The more specific you can get about how you are feeling, the better. If you are angry, what's under the layer of anger? Is it hurt? Sadness? Betrayal? Ask yourself:

What am I feeling? I notice the feeling of _____.

Is this feeling mine or someone else's?

Do I want to keep this feeling or can I let it go?

Is this feeling being magnified by the reactions of others?

Would it be helpful to talk to and share with someone you trust?

Feelings are your body's messengers. They tell you to pay attention, because there is something important you need to address. If you get curious about your emotions and listen to what they have to say, you'll be able to work through them and feel less overwhelmed. You can make friends with your emotions instead of trying avoid them or make them go away.

"I didn't think it would work, but I took a breath and started noticing what was going on in my head, and I was able to move on."

–High school student, age 17

• • •

In some instances, thoughts of self-harm and dying emerge when you are experiencing prolonged negative emotions and feel overwhelmed. When stuck in these feelings, it is almost impossible to gain perspective or see the way out on your own. If you ever have thoughts about suicide and death, reach out instead of isolating. Be with someone. Reach out to a parent, friend, teacher, counselor, or call the National Suicide Hotline at **1-800-273-8255.** The pain is real, and you deserve to be heard.

● ● ●

You matter.
We see you.

WHAT IS THIS EMOTIONAL SAFETY YOU SPEAK OF?

When people don't feel emotionally safe, they are more likely to feel anxious, depressed, and lonely. When you don't feel safe emotionally, it's much harder to use the thinking and reasoning part of your brain that helps you decide if you are okay. You land in **fight, flight, or freeze** mode which floods you with emotions and stress hormones.

This heightened state of emotions makes it more difficult to learn or process new information. You aren't able to think as clearly and often assume you are the only one feeling this way. Your feelings take over, and then your brain starts generating more negative ways of thinking. It's easy to believe these negative thoughts are true, because your emotional state makes them "feel" true. You start to develop many more inaccurate and unhealthy patterns of thinking, which only worsen negativity.

Emotional safety consists of being able to recognize our feelings, to allow ourselves to experience our feelings, and to connect with others to share our feelings and needs.

● ● ●

WE GOTTA START TALKING ...

We know that TALKING makes you feel BETTER. Talking with others about what you experience creates connection and shared understanding. Our clients were often surprised that when they talked with their friends about feeling anxious and depressed, many of them were experiencing the same feelings. When you realize you are not alone, you also realize that you are not defective. Your feelings are a normal reaction to hard things.

Unfortunately, some adults can be a little slower to recognize and talk about emotional difficulties. Many in that generation were taught to keep their emotions private and that showing emotions is a sign of weakness. Adults may not be fully aware of their own feelings and are also trying to make sense of what is going on. Life is hard and confusing for everyone. Some adults may feel less able to cope effectively, and in turn, less equipped to be a resource for their kids.

When you hold onto big feelings, you may notice physical symptoms: racing heart, stomach pain, muscle tension, and headaches. Surprise! These are the body's reaction to mental and emotional stress. The mind-body connection is real. So, when you feel those chronic physical symptoms, talk to someone about what you're feeling.

Being able to relate to each other is the first step in shifting the way we see and feel the world.

● ● ●

Social distancing (mostly) sucked!

Many activities — sports, theater, clubs, church — were canceled during the start of the pandemic. Many are still not the same. These activities, however, are necessary to grow a strong sense of self and belonging and to develop a healthy, balanced life.

Your generation is not making excuses or being dramatic. The need for social connection is critical at this stage of your life.

Due to the social restrictions, your generation missed out on opportunities to feel a sense of belonging and to practice being part of a group. Both of these are necessary to build important social skills that you will use later in life. As teens, it is normal to want to spend more time with your friends than with your parents.

Many were not able to test healthy boundaries. For example, some seniors reported not feeling equipped to leave for college or to go out on their own, because they didn't have the real-life experiences they needed to feel successful. Some struggled so much that they had to come home from college.

For some, the initial social restrictions were a temporary relief from the constant pressures of social situations. Although this relief may have felt good for a few days or weeks, ultimately the lack of socializing in person proved to be unhealthy, especially for kids and teens with pre-existing anxiety and depression. Socializing often becomes harder or feels intimidating the less practice you have. Simple things, like making plans with friends or ordering coffee, can feel out of place and surprisingly uncomfortable.

Even now, some kids and teens have gotten so used to being more isolated and socially disconnected that they feel more awkward around their peers and unsure how to connect.

Awkwardness is a normal part of social interactions. It is more so now, as you get used to being around each other again.

● ● ●

And so did re-entry.

It was exciting when things started to open back up. Humans are social creatures who need people and thrive on a sense of belonging. Many mistakenly assumed they could jump right back into life and socializing with others. However, social worlds have shifted and continue to shift. Many are still trying to find their place and are confused because they expected to instantly feel happy. This unrealistic expectation led many to feel defective, as if there was something wrong with them.

It is no surprise that anxiety and depression continue to rise. The ongoing emotional and social struggles are confusing for all ages, even your parents and grandparents. People are still searching for their "normal." The truth is you can't go back, and that is not a bad thing. You will find a new normal. People learn and grow from hard times. Changing your perspective and expectations is vital to combat anxiety and depression.

Changes and transitions are never easy. Discomfort is a natural part of learning to adapt to new, unfamiliar situations.

• • •

Limits on socializing can disrupt the development of essential coping skills. Your brain needs to feel connected to others to gain perspective on emotional experiences, make sense of the world, and learn life skills. Unfortunately, society often praises being independent and self-made. Many equate being strong with doing things on their own, without relying on others. In reality, strength comes from having the support of others. Interdependence and relying on others, even same-age peers, offers individuals greater balance and allows people to need people. This is exactly how brains are designed! People need each other, particularly during challenging times. Life is full of so many hard things, even without a pandemic. You are only as strong as your bonds with others.

Colleague and psychiatrist Dr. Eric Kulick provides a very helpful analogy. "The idea of full independence is like saying someone should live without oxygen." Getting your needs met is not something you can do on your own! It's not only okay to need people, but it is actually necessary for your physical, mental, and emotional health.

When you share your struggles and successes with others, you understand yourself better, and others understand you better. That understanding leads to connection. Humans are social creatures, after all.

As you ease back into social situations, we hope you realize the importance of staying connected.

A 17-year old high school student sat down for lunch surrounded by his closest friends and said, "At least I'm not having a panic attack today." That was the opening that his friends needed to all disclose they were struggling with panic and anxiety. They were shocked because they had no idea they were all struggling.

● ● ●

Social media made everything worse (duh)!

The Netflix documentary *The Social Dilemma*, released in January 2020, highlighted social media as a major contributor to a decline in youths' mental health prior to the onset of the pandemic. Social distancing, in combination with the need for social connection, further intensified reliance on social media. People are spending more time on social media, watching videos, and gaming. Technology feels like the way to stay connected with friends and pass the time. Unfortunately, social media as a platform has grown wildly with little regulation, resulting in many unintended consequences that have proven to be detrimental to your mental health.

Social media makes it easier to be mean, bully, and spread rumors. People are quick to respond or share information without really thinking. Things got a lot worse for vulnerable people who were targeted. Social media is also the most common way you end up comparing yourself to others. Unfortunately, social media makes it easy to perceive yourself or a situation in a way that simply ISN'T REAL or doesn't accurately represent the whole story. It's easy to compare yourself to what is on social media, without considering the source of the data, and find yourself lacking. Everyone has a natural tendency to compare. It has become a deeply unhealthy habit ingrained in the algorithms of social media to keep us coming back for more.

> "The pandemic acted as a catalyst for social media and accelerated people's reliance on it."
>
> –Dr. Eric Kulick

Recognizing the fallacies of social media and evaluating the source of your thoughts helps you separate fact from fiction. Consider these problematic assumptions:

- Forgetting that a person might be struggling because she just posted a picture of herself on Instagram looking happy. The reality is people post what makes them feel good and look good.

- Forgetting that YouTube shows are not real and have been cropped, edited, filtered, and staged. They are highlight reels.

- Thinking "I am fat" because of pictures of others who look "amazing" and forgetting that many people use filters to make themselves look better. They often have to take multiple pictures to get one that puts them in the best light.

- Thinking "Life is easier for him" because of a story he posted on social media. In reality, the story may have been fabricated or enhanced to make the person feel better about himself.

- Thinking "I should be happy" because many TV shows depict happiness as a goal, and issues seem to resolve quickly. In reality, happiness is a feeling. No feeling lasts forever, even happiness. ALL feelings come and go. Furthermore, it usually takes more than 30 minutes or an hour (the length of a show) to resolve challenging situations.

- Thinking "I must be stupid or not good enough" because social media makes most things look so easy. It only looks easy because things are practiced repeatedly until perfected for posting.

- Thinking "I should have a huge group of followers or I'm not likable." Followers don't equal friends and should not be a measure of your self-worth.

As you can see, turning to social media when vulnerable can be a lethal combination for your self-esteem and for mental health.

Many parents don't have any idea what it is like growing up connected to social media. It is really hard to fully understand something you haven't experienced. Even though explaining your world to the adults around you might feel annoying, pointless, or uncomfortable, they cannot know what it's like living during a pandemic with social media and data overload, unless you tell them. Adults might remember feeling insecure and left out as a teenager, but it's almost impossible to grasp how social media greatly exaggerates and prolongs these feelings. For example, older generations were able to take a break from the emotional pain of feeling left out or bullied. Your generation doesn't have the luxury of taking a break, unless you disconnect from your friends on social media. If you are on your phone, you will see pictures of friends and classmates, seemingly having fun on every app you open.

Initially, adults were more understanding of the distress caused by the pandemic. Sadly, we notice that much of this tolerance and grace has been lost. The pandemic leaves people feeling fatigued, leading to ripples of anxiety and irritability all around us.

• • •

IS ONLINE SCHOOL YOUR JAM OR YOUR NEMESIS?

Online school was a totally abrupt and unique experience for all ages and affected everyone differently. People found themselves unable to settle into a rhythm, because things were constantly changing even when schools re-opened. In online school, you miss out on the energy of the classroom, time with friends, ability to ask questions, and motivation to work. If you struggle with attention or don't consider yourself a self-starter, online school likely added another level of stress. Even some traditionally high-achieving students experienced a massive dip in their GPAs and confidence.

The struggle continues because school is still not the same. It's harder to focus. The fun parts of school are still missing. It's harder to find your people with masks and schedules that are put in place to expose fewer students. Feeling alone and stuck at school can make it harder to know where to begin. This is not surprising. Research shows that you cannot learn effectively when anxiety is heightened because access to the thinking parts of the brain is limited. It is no wonder that many feel inadequate or defective, not living up to or functioning at pre-pandemic standards.

Faculty and staff at schools are working hard. Many are also understandably feeling overwhelmed and out of gas. The pressure for teachers to focus on physical safety and catching students back up academically leaves little space to consider students' emotional needs.

Feeling pressure creates stress and can lead to panic, self-doubt, and difficulty breaking down or starting even simple tasks. If you are overwhelmed or stuck, what you really need is someone to help prioritize and break down tasks into manageable steps. This is NOT A WEAKNESS, but the new reality of this world.

Take charge. Talk to yourself like you would a friend. Words matter, whether talking to yourself or to others. Remind yourself that you are doing the best you can. The road to success is always under construction. Developing perseverance and consistent, disciplined action are key factors to keeping you on that road. Hang in there, and remember you actually learn the most from hard things! No one with a lot of character hasn't had their fair share of hard things.

"At the end of the day, your first friend is and always remains yourself."

–High school student, age 15

• • •

So, what now?

Amid chaos and difficulties, there is also benefit. Challenges can bring us together and often serve as catalysts for growth and change. We have been impressed by our clients during this time of global pandemic. You speak the truth and are steadfast. You embrace mental health and are change makers.

We hope you realize how strong you are. Have faith in yourself when you're in difficult situations. Know you have what you need inside you. Be on the lookout for thoughts that are unrealistic and overly harsh. Tell yourself, "I don't need them," or "Thanks, but not helpful." It's easy to blame yourself for not feeling motivated or inspired. Remember, there is a lot is out of your control. Be gentle with yourself.

SPEAK UP! Use your voice, and let the adults around you know what it is like growing up in this generation. Each generation faces different struggles and challenges, and that is life! Sharing and being vulnerable is the only way to move forward.

A deeper dive

Thanks for hanging with us. If you want to learn more about how your body and mind work and what to do to keep them working best, keep reading!

● ● ●

YIKES! THE SAFETY CONTROL CENTER.

Let's get started.
Step one in tackling
anxiety is understanding
where it comes from and how it works.
The safety control center part of the brain
senses danger and keeps you safe by cautioning you to avoid the
danger. It's great at setting off an alarm that screams, "Pay attention!"
We call it the YIKES feeling. The foundation of this alarm system
developed out of the need for survival millions of years ago.

These days, brains are much more complex, but they still work in
some of the same ways as they did for early human ancestors. One of
the biggest things brains have in common with early human ancestors
is the amygdala. The amygdala has a BIG name for a reason! This
almond-shaped part of the brain may be small, but it stores one of
the brain's most important systems — **the safety control center.** It's
the on-off switch for emotions, especially anxiety and frustration.

When the amygdala activates the alarm, it limits the thinking part of your brain and relies on reactions — **fight, flight, or freeze.** Your body does amazing things to keep you safe, take action, and even save your life or someone else's. For example, if the fire alarm goes off in your house:

- You will feel a surge of adrenaline throughout your body.
- Your heart will start beating faster to get fuel to your muscles.
- You'll start breathing faster and shallower to get more oxygen so you'll be ready to run fast.
- Your muscles fill with energy ready to fight or take flight, making them tense and sometimes shaky.
- Your digestive system is interrupted so your body can use the energy. This disruption can make you feel nauseous or like you need to race to the bathroom.

All these things will give you temporary superhuman speed and strength to get out of the house! Your brain and body are powerful and know what is needed to keep you safe!

The threats we perceive today are different from those thousands of years ago. The brain still sounds the alarm for perceived physical threats, but now triggers the alarm for perceived social and emotional threats too. The reactions to threats have also evolved and look more like this:

FIGHT
Throw a fit, argue, blame others, or do whatever you can to stay safe.

FLIGHT
Run away or avoid whatever is triggering anxiety.

FREEZE
Shut down and withdraw, often not communicating at all.

This emotional safety alarm is often quite helpful and supports making decisions in combination with our thinking brain. Here are some examples:

- Feeling like a person is making an unsafe decision and deciding to not go along with them
- Your gut telling you not to post a picture to social media
- Deciding to temporarily mute someone on social media who is upsetting you
- Being bullied and deciding to reach out to others and find support
- Recognizing that someone is not respecting your boundaries and speaking up
- Feeling invalidated and seeking out new friendships

The amygdala can get confused and then tries to overprotect you. It sounds the alarm too frequently or too loudly and gets stuck. The alarm might sound when thinking about something that didn't seem to go well in the past or something that might happen in the future. It will keep you focused on trying to solve an unsolvable problem. Ironically, when the amygdala is overprotective about situations that are not actual threats, anxiety spreads like wildfire and takes over. Anxiety latches on to the worst-case scenario, making it all about you, and telling you that you can't handle things. You get lost in your thoughts and believe them to be true, even though they are simply passing ideas — not reality.

Enough with the stress! It's making me sick.

Mental health and physical safety are interconnected, and our body doesn't like to give up! If you try to ignore unwanted emotions, the body eventually takes over and sends signals like headaches, stomach aches, numbness, and tingly feelings in an attempt to get your attention. The mind and body often work together without conscious awareness, which is even confusing for adults. As a result, sometimes people may be quick to dismiss physical concerns as minor or default to thinking that you're making excuses to get out of something.

Ignoring or dismissing feelings makes them bigger, which creates more physical symptoms. This can cause weird illnesses or symptoms that even doctors don't understand. Likewise, if the energy building up to keep you safe doesn't have anywhere to go, you may act in ways that make situations worse! You might inadvertently push away friends and caring adults. For example, people are not as likely to be supportive if they feel attacked, and the message can get lost.

In reality, physical symptoms are a built-in emotional thermometer coming from your safety control center. If you don't understand how the mind-body connection works, the symptoms can feel terrifying. If you fear these physical signals, the alarm sounds louder, triggering more symptoms. By becoming more aware of physical sensations and acknowledging what's happening, you can better determine whether your body is sending a false or exaggerated alarm or whether action is needed to solve a problem. Your body then has what it needs to move through the anxiety.

Hello panic. I don't like you.

Sometimes, your amygdala gets stuck on high alert for no apparent reason, and you experience sudden, intense physical changes (e.g., heart racing, breathing too fast, stomach aches, shaky muscles). Even though it's a false alarm, your overly effective safety control center can make you THINK and FEEL that your body is doing something unsafe.

Then you might think, "What if this happens when I'm at class or away from my parents?" or "Why is this happening?" or "What if I can't get the feeling to go away?" This type of thinking makes the fear grow. Before you know it, you develop a fear of feeling the fear. This fear can keep you from doing things you enjoy, like learning at school, spending time with friends, reaching out to others, or enjoying activities. The pandemic can limit opportunities to be with people who can help you feel better.

Thanks panic. I don't need you.

Once you recognize the panic feeling and let your mind and body know it's a false alarm, the physical sensations will decrease on their own. The goal is not to get rid of the panic, but to allow it to pass without fear.

Here are some ideas to help you work through panic:

- Tell yourself, "I am experiencing panic. False alarm. It is uncomfortable but not dangerous. I am safe." Ground yourself by noticing and naming 5 things you can see, 4 things you can feel, 3 things you can hear, 2 things you can smell, and 1 thing you can taste.

- Do infinity breathing by tracing an infinity symbol (∞). Start in the center, trace one half breathing in, pause at center, and breathe out as you trace the other half. Do this 10 times. Most people think breathing doesn't work because they expect it to make the panic feeling disappear. In reality, breathing helps interrupt your system so it can reset.

- Carry a smooth stone in your pocket. The stone is cool to the touch, so you can focus on it's texture. It's easy to have available and doesn't call attention to yourself.

- Change your scenery and go for a walk, paying special attention the physical feeling of walking and the scenery around you.

- Ask the counselor for a "fast pass," so you can leave the classroom any time. Go to the restroom and run your hands under water, or splash cold water on your face.

- Listen to your favorite song, focusing on all the notes and the words.

When you are prepared with a plan in place, you might expect panic but not dread it. Panic will be less scary because you know what it is, what to do, and that panic always passes. Be patient and kind to yourself and others, as you learn to conquer the fear of the fear!

SOCIAL MEDIA: WHAT'S THE REAL DEAL?

The real deal is that social media capitalizes off of impulsivity and instant gratification to keep people hooked and coming back for more. Repetitive distractions from notifications literally make your brain struggle more with attention and concentration. Unfortunately, the more you are on social media, the less aware you become of its impact on you.

You are the first generation to truly grow up in the age of social media, meaning you have to be the ones figuring out what is healthy for you and what is not. It's unrealistic to think you can just stop social media, gaming, or watching videos. Learn how to become a good consumer of technology. Don't just leave it up to the adults to make the rules.

Consider these points when sharing or posting:

- Is this my information to share? Is it necessary?
- How would I feel if someone shared this about me?
- Would I say this in real life?
- Does sharing this information fit with who you want to be?
- Ultimately, would you want your grandma to see what you posted?

Set your own boundaries:

- Experiment. Take a break from a specific app or apps, person, or group to see how you feel. Riding out the urge to obsessively check your phone is a hard habit to break. You might be surprised at how liberating it may feel to disconnect.
- Pay attention to how you feel after watching a video or reading posts, and let those feelings guide your decisions.
- Mute notifications or set your phone aside so you are not distracted all the time.

You're right. Friends matter (duh)!

Restrictions to socialization can disrupt social development and the understanding of what healthy friendships look like. No one has a million friends and followers. It's also not realistic or healthy to believe that you will always be invited to everything. Adults struggle with this too. All friendships naturally wax and wane. Sometimes, you outgrow certain people. That's okay, as long as you are kind about it. You will never regret taking the high road, but you may regret being unkind. No one can be liked by EVERYONE. One authentic friendship is worth more than a zillion likes.

Friends matter so much, and everyone is hurting. People are raw and vulnerable. Humans are social creatures designed to care about each other in a community. It's easy to get caught up in trying to save or fix each other, but that's an impossible task. Anxiety and depression love company, which makes it easy to unknowingly absorb and spread others' feelings.

Fixing or absorbing feelings prevents a person from learning how to experience and sit with uncomfortable feelings. Instead, show compassion by listening and acknowledging, but set a limit on how long you'll spend discussing it. Excessive attention to feelings actually makes them grow instead of allowing them to pass. Be a friend and do activities you enjoy together. Go on a drive, take a walk, play cards, watch a movie, listen to music — simply doing regular activities provides comfort. With time, you and your friends will learn that you can handle a lot more than you think you can!

With the cumulative stress of being your age, some people may think about death to stop the emotional pain. If you are concerned about ANYONE, talking it through with a trusted adult is a MUST. They can assess the severity and provide the right resources. When you come from a place of caring, no one will hold it against you.

Retrain your brain. Yeah, that's a thing.

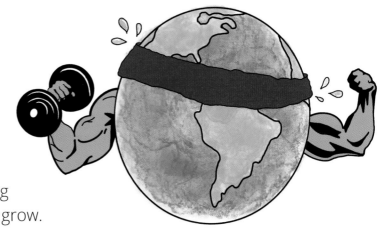

Here's the BEST NEWS!
The brain is like a
muscle and can
change over time!
In fact, working through
hard things and learning
how to tolerate distressing
emotions helps the brain grow.
If you can recognize bad patterns,
you can create new ones that work better for you. You can develop
new, stronger frameworks for figuring out future relationships and
experiences. Instead of constantly beating yourself up for bad habits,
you can feel empowered about your ability to discover new habits.
Your brain's ability to change, grow, and adapt through experience is
referred to as **neuroplasticity.** Essentially neurons, the nerve cells
in the brain, reorganize and regroup to form new pathways based
on life experience. If you increase your awareness of what helps you
feel better or worse, you can focus more energy on strengthening
the good parts.

Strengthening your brain works the same way as building your
biceps. It needs daily exercise! You can grow the parts of your brain
that help you understand and work through your feelings. You can
train different parts of your brain to work together or help them work
together more effectively.

Changing and growing your brain takes patience and lots of practice.
Practice makes progress. It also requires working on these things
when you are in a calm and rational state.

Let's talk about ways you can grow different parts of your brain.

YOUR SCHOOL BRAIN: Most kids who do really well in school spend a lot of time reading and practicing at home. You may not be aware of the time and effort they spend on schoolwork. They also tend to ask for help when needed. Honestly, the smartest people know they don't know everything and embrace asking for help. Growing your school brain also involves setting yourself up for success. Do things such as create a plan for getting homework done each day, decrease distractions by putting your phone on airplane mode, join a study group, go to the library, and maintain a system of organization. You can also strengthen your school brain by seeing tests as a tool, rather than as an evaluation of your "smartness," ability, or worth. Tests provide students and teachers feedback about what they have learned and what they need to spend more time learning. When it comes to tests, focus on showing what you do know versus worrying about what you might not know. Likewise, just because something is hard or takes longer to do does not mean you're not good at it. Learning takes work!

YOUR SOCIAL BRAIN: Everyone feels anxious reaching out, even kids and adults who look super confident! Start small. Leave the house. Standing straighter, holding your head up, and putting your phone down all allow for eye contact and lets others know you are approachable. Start with a head nod and smile (even under your mask because you can still see the smile in your eyes). Setting goals for saying hi, waving, or starting conversations helps create a mindset to look for opportunities, rather than waiting for others to approach you. Be yourself instead of trying to figure out what you're supposed to do to fit in. Being genuine is the basis for real friendships. Shared activities, such as watching movies, shopping, baking, crafting, or watching sports, make conversations easier. Rather than assuming the worst, see what happens when you reach out. Not every interaction will be what you wanted it to be. That's OK. Focus on progress. Expect that it might take longer than you want to feel reconnected or to find your people.

YOUR CALM BRAIN: Ironically, the calm part of the brain only gets stronger by trying and practicing strategies when you are calm. Practicing helps your body get used to what calm feels like and makes it easier to get that calm feeling back when you are upset. You are building muscle memory! Dr. Bruce Perry, a famous neuroscientist and expert on trauma, has proven with brain scans how rhythmic movement and connection help activate the calming parts of the brain. Finding your calm can be done in *so* many ways, such as: practicing yoga, walking, throwing a ball, coloring, rowing, riding a bike, dancing, listening to music, swinging in a hammock, singing, playing frisbee golf, shooting baskets, journaling, blowing bubbles, hiking, and just sitting in nature with friends. Let the adults know what works for you, so you both know the plan when you are upset. What works for them may not work for you and vice versa. They won't know if you don't tell them. Exercise is an easy and essential step in growing the calm part of our brain, because it allows you to let go of the negative energy that builds up in your body when distressed. Daily movement benefits your mental health as much as your physical health. It's like your daily stress-release valve, so make it happen. Start small but aim for at least 20 minutes per day. Do things that are simple and fun to make it easier to build a lasting habit.

No matter what part of the brain you're working on, remember it takes time to create new patterns. Brains are hard-wired to stick with what's familiar, even if it's not working. Training your brain takes time, patience, practice, and hope, just like a marathon runner. The runner has to build endurance and wouldn't be ready if he or she hadn't run consistently for more than a year. Be kind to yourself in the process — we promise it will get easier!

● ● ●

KNOW AND GROW YOUR STRONG.

Building any muscle, whether in our brain or body, takes a lot of work, discipline, and dedication. This is true for everyone. Everyone has strengths and talents.

Society used to focus primarily on only one kind of smart, often measured by an IQ test or grades. We now know that gifts, such as emotional intelligence, social skills, and creativity are just as IMPORTANT. In fact, they are often a more realistic predictor of happiness and "success" than the ability to obtain high test scores. Everyone has gifts! It may seem that some find them easier and earlier. Don't stop searching. Yours is out there!

The best way to grow confidence and become who you were meant to be is by focusing on what is going well. Nurture and embrace your strengths. Yes, you need support for challenges, but keep growing your gifts and talents. Imagine you're a lawn that needs care. You can pull the weeds (i.e., the things causing problems), but if you don't water and plant grass, the weeds resurface. By focusing on nurturing strengths and talents, there's less opportunity for the weeds to take root again. Some of you may be thinking, "This sounds great, but I haven't discovered my talents, and I have no idea where to begin." Pay attention to what fills you up and what is going well. Invest in yourself. This takes practice.

Forge ahead. Make new paths.

Neuroscience shows YOU CAN overcome hardships and grow into a stronger, healthier, more confident person. You learn the most about yourself and what truly matters when you go through hard times or fail. Neuroplasticity, or the ability for your brain to change, inspires hope to persevere when faced with challenges.

In the book *What Happened to You,* Dr. Bruce Perry and Oprah Winfrey illustrate how the brain develops certain protective patterns during challenging or traumatic experiences. Once these experiences have passed, however, these patterns may no longer be necessary and can become harmful. For example, if you were bullied, you may have become quieter and more withdrawn, while trying to avoid attention from the bully. Once the situation resolves, these same behaviors will interfere with making meaningful connections to other people.

The key is recognizing which behaviors and beliefs are unhealthy, even if they feel familiar. It's common to need help identifying different, healthier ways of doing things. By giving yourself permission to explore change, your mind becomes more open to discovering new patterns. Before you know it, you are on a new path that works better for you and your individual needs.

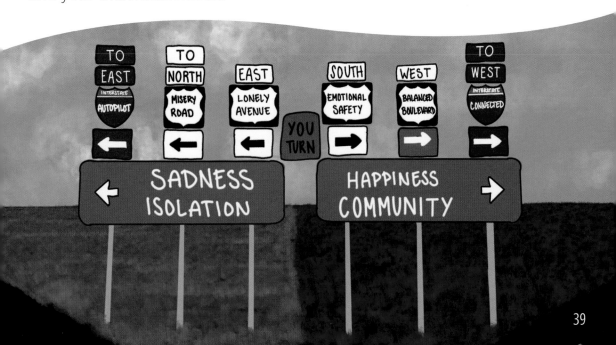

LEAN ON AND LEARN FROM EACH OTHER.

Now that you know about the mind/body connection and neuroplasticity, it's time to introduce another important concept — **co-regulation**. Co-regulation means your brain can sense and mirror the state of the people around you. Have you ever walked into a room and felt immediately stressed or suddenly calm or happy? This is what Dr. Bruce Perry calls **emotional contagion.**

So how does this all work? Your brain's blueprints are neuronal networks (information superhighways) that resemble spiderwebs. Different networks link up with others, which is why one feeling can trigger another feeling or memory. Many associations are buried deeply and triggered automatically by your sensory experiences, such as smells and sounds, without your awareness. As a result, you might be caught off guard and unsure of what's happening and how to respond.

If you are unclear why you're distressed or what to do, finding a calm person is a helpful first step. Dr. Perry describes this as **catching their calm** and is the essence of co-regulation. When you experience distress in a safe place with a safe person, your brain can then access higher, thinking parts of the brain needed to gain insight and make healthy decisions. Seeking support is the key to finding balance, calm, and perspective. People need people, especially "their" people. Now that you know this, you can focus your energy on fostering relationships that help you become the best version of yourself.

Hello perspective.

The pandemic magnifies and complicates the stress of being your age. There is so much changing in your brain, body, and life. It's easier to do well when things are more certain, and you know what to expect. The lack of clear, stable expectations creates a perfect storm for losing perspective. Making mistakes often feels unacceptable. If something doesn't go well, you blame yourself. Making mistakes is a natural and expected part of figuring yourself out. In fact, making mistakes and going through hard things allow you to develop perspective, empathy, and wisdom.

Once you are able to look at the big picture and see what is real, your perspective shifts. You are more likely to take a chance on yourself and develop more confidence. Gaining perspective requires pausing when difficult situations and feelings arise. This allows you to notice your thoughts and feelings without judgment.

Here are tips to help gain perspective:

- Is this a situation where there isn't a right or best answer?
- Is this problem worth my time and energy?
- How might I have contributed to the problem or situation?
- How might someone else have contributed to the problem or situation?
- How much did the situation itself actually contribute to the problem?
- What can I control?
- Will this matter 4 weeks, 4 months, or 4 years from now?
- Do I need to do something about the problem, or is it an unfortunate situation that I can let go and move on?

Find your balance.

The start of the pandemic forced a slowing down, or built-in reprieve, from the busyness of life. Busyness was no longer a badge of honor or an expectation for the first time in this generation. As the world tries to get back to "normal," it makes sense to question which parts of life matter the most and are worth your time and energy.

For example, sleep is an essential part of finding balance and reducing anxiety. When exhausted, you go on auto-pilot, have less capacity to cope, and are more insecure. An over-scheduled world that doesn't allow for adequate sleep sets us up for failure. Society's expectations make it hard to figure out the work/school-life balance. It is SO HARD to say no when you feel the pressure to do it all.

Just like you can "catch the calm" from others, you can also catch distress and frustration from those around you. Finding balance includes learning how to OBSERVE but not ABSORB. This means that you can become aware of and empathize with someone else's thoughts or feelings without absorbing them and letting them take over. When you take on the emotional current of those around you, it clouds intuition and creates confusion. Ask yourself, "Whose emotion is this? Is this mine? Do I need to take it on? Can I allow it to float by?"

Be mindful.

The pandemic, like most challenging life experiences, makes it virtually impossible to be present with so much information and uncertainty. Consider whether gathering more information is either necessary or helpful. Who or what is the source of your information, and is it reliable? EVERYONE needs help with this right now.

If you feel overwhelmed, chances are that your thoughts are not staying in the present, but rather reviewing the past or predicting a terrible future. **Mindfulness** essentially means paying attention to the present without judgment. You can plan ahead but don't need to worry ahead. So, if you're in math class, then think about math. If you're having a conversation, put your phone down and focus on the person and conversation. Being present makes it easier to follow the conversation and know what to say.

Be where your feet are. Do one task at a time and focus on what you CAN control in the moment. Put your phone down and turn off notifications more often. It is NOT normal or healthy to be available 24/7, even if you are "free."

Try breathing between activities. As you finish an activity or task, thank yourself. Appreciating that a task is complete allows you to feel more satisfied and motivated to move to the next thing. The ability to be mindful is key to gaining self-control and feeling a sense of peace.

The best moments happen when you aren't looking for them but when you are content enough to see them.

• • •

DITCH THE DAILY GRIND.

It's easy to live life on auto-pilot — essentially going through the motions. It's time to go from auto-pilot to manual override and ditch the daily grind!

Just because you CAN do something does not mean you SHOULD. You aren't superhuman and really cannot "do it all," despite the pressure you may feel from society. Setting too many goals or setting goals too high produces thoughts that set you up to feel like a failure.

A high school student wanted to take five AP classes during the pandemic; however, he also expressed that he often felt barely afloat, and that if he didn't feel that way, he clearly wasn't doing enough. After reflection about his wants and needs versus society's, he came to this conclusion, *"Our brain just wants familiarity. We don't want to change, and we push away whatever makes us uncomfortable. But it is possible to change. Everyone is going through similar problems. And everything — school, college prep, and life in general — is different right now because of the pandemic. I DON'T have to fit society's standards."*

Figuring out what you want and need rather than what you "should" do helps you feel more in control of the outcome. PASSION IS PURPOSE!

- What activities lead to a sense of fulfillment, enjoyment, or productivity?
- What sparks passion and gives your life purpose?
- What qualities do you want to define you?
- Where do you see opportunities for growth?
- What do you do that helps you feel better in the long run?

Knowing what you value helps you make the right choices for you. Understanding what you value will help you grow and feel fulfilled. Give it some thought, then take action.

The future is yours!

BREAK THIS DOWN FOR ME.

We've covered a lot of information so far. We want to leave you with actionable items that will move you along the path from surviving to vibing. The following strategies help strengthen your brain and build the foundations so you can navigate any of life's challenges, pandemic or not.

01. Leave the comfort zone. Doing challenging things can change your brain for the better. Scaffolding, or breaking things down into manageable steps, can boost success, build self-esteem, and instill a sense of mastery — all of which fuel motivation. By challenging yourself and going outside your comfort zone, consider these actions as experiments. Be curious, and see what happens — anxiety says it won't be good, but you'll likely be relieved and surprised that anxiety didn't know what it was talking about. And, it gets easier each time.

02. Exercise. Research shows that 20 minutes a day of cardio with an elevated heart rate can enhance mood. YouTube videos, exercise apps, working out with a buddy, and setting goals helps you commit to developing a habit of exercise. Any movement is good, even five minutes of stretching, dancing to a song, walking to get the mail, or taking a quick bike ride around the block. Whatever it is, find something you enjoy doing, so you're more likely to keep doing it.

03. Prioritize sleep. Sleep is essential. Sleep is EVERYTHING. Set a regular sleep and wake time and shut down electronics at least 60 minutes before falling asleep (or at least put it in night mode!). Reserve your bed for sleep. Think through your day to recall the good parts and what you're looking forward to next day. Listen to music, a podcast, or an app designed to help you sleep. Many find weighted blankets help them ease into sleep by helping them feel cozier, more comfortable, and safe.

04. Eat well and drink water. Healthy eating and hydration are essential. Bring a water bottle and use it. Food is fuel. Don't forget to eat the good stuff and have snacks accessible.

05. Connect with nature, rhythm, and movement. Activities involving nature, rhythm, and movement can settle you. The mere sounds and textures of nature are healing. Nature is a great source of natural vitamin D. Low vitamin D levels significantly impact your mood and energy. Being outside also allows you to feel free and like a kid again. Nature provides endless opportunities for exploring and healing.

06. Start each day fresh. Every day, get up, shower, and put on clean clothes, even if it's another pair of sweat pants. You will feel better, and it's a signal to your body that you are ready for a new day. Choose clothes that make you feel good about yourself. You don't need to dress to impress. Simply dress like you care.

07. Try a bulleted brain dump. When your brains are overwhelmed with thoughts and feelings, it means there is too much in your head. It is often helpful to write out your thoughts and feelings, literally getting them out of your head. Writing helps condense and see thoughts and feelings more clearly, so you can evaluate them with less judgment and emotion.

08. Find your calm with others. Surround yourself with good people, and good things will happen. Find that person who brings out your calm and knows how to help just by looking at you. Sometimes, it's a sibling, coach, parent, or a close friend — anyone who can help you regain that calm by their presence. Know that you can also be that calm for others. One of the best ways to help someone through distressing emotions is to sit quietly with them without offering advice or judgment.

09. Find your voice. Putting words to what you're experiencing helps you make sense of it. Talking about or writing out your thoughts and feelings helps you gain perspective. Use art, journaling, music, or texting another way to express yourself if talking feels too overwhelming. Start somewhere. You deserve to be heard.

10. Focus on the good parts. Because happiness comes and goes like all feelings. Although brains are hardwired to fixate on the negative, you can actively and consciously practice focusing on the positives too! One of our favorite activities, especially before bed, is the 3, 2, 1 exercise:

- Three things that put a smile on your face or that you appreciated
- Two things to look forward to the next day (Be specific. If it's hard to think of something, add an activity to your day that you enjoy or makes you feel productive.)
- One good thing about yourself (a quality, appearance, something others might like about you, what makes you feel proud)

11. Adopt a growth-oriented mindset. A growth mindset is one that gives you permission to be imperfect, to mess up, and to learn from your mistakes. It allows you to take risks and move outside your comfort zones to become who you were meant to be. Feedback is a gift. A word of encouragement during a failure is worth more than an hour of praise after a success. Help build each other up. Tapping into your growth mindset, boosts self-esteem, reduces your inner critic, and improves your confidence.

12. Seek therapy. Therapy is a helpful, non-biased outlet and a space for growth. Therapy should be unique to each individual and his or her specific needs. When choosing a therapist, it is important to feel a safe connection. If it doesn't seem like a good fit, find someone who is! Find someone who gives you a voice and doesn't rush you. Trust us, if it's the right person, it is amazing!

13. Meditate. Meditation, in simple words, helps your brain slow down, become more aware of where you are in the moment, and increase your focus. Meditation is like a pause switch that settles your central nervous system. You are able to notice what you are thinking, feeling, and experiencing and then redirect your attention and energy where it is needed. Meditation creates calm and decreases stress.

14. Be kind and helpful. Being kind helps you make connections, get out of your own head, and spread positive emotions. Reach out to others. Volunteer. Write a letter to an elderly relative. Thinking of others will flood you with good feelings, and you'll make the world better in the process. Random acts of kindness feel good. Do them often.

Only you can figure out which strategies work best for you to grow and change your brain. It won't be the same plan as your friend's since everyone is uniquely wired. Be curious. Be adventurous. Be patient. You got this!

You are a strong generation who deserve tools,
validation, and a voice.

Carron and Caroline teamed up to write this book to help you
make sense of all that is going on and help you build resilience.
A team approach is always more impactful and rewarding. Our
journey together has only reinforced this belief. We will release
more books in *The Invisible Riptide* series. We hope you enjoy
them as much as we love writing them.

For more information, reading, and resources please visit
www.theinvisibleriptide.com.

● ● ●

About the Authors

Carron Montgomery, MSCP, LPC, RPT is a Licensed Professional Counselor, Registered Play Therapist and Level II EMDR therapist. Carron utilizes a client-centered approach that includes the importance of collaborating with each client's team of professionals and primary caregivers. At the beginning of the pandemic, Carron saw a huge need for education and support that was not being addressed. She trained local school counselors and began writing to provide additional resources to the community and as a voice for her clients.

Caroline Danda, PHD, LP is a clinical psychologist who specializes in working with children and adolescents with anxiety, depression, and other emotional or behavioral regulation problems. She loves working with children and teens who have "big emotions." She has a passion for normalizing mental and emotional health and helping youth and their families not only resolve current challenges but also develop foundational skills for thriving.

Acknowledgments

This book would not have been possible without our supportive husbands, families, and larger networks of friends who are family — you know who you are! To say it has taken a village to write this book is an understatement. To our parents who modeled and instilled a work ethic and appreciation for life, your wisdom is evident through the book. A special thank you to our mothers, who are examples of unconditional love and support.

The creation of *The Invisible Riptide* series and this book was fueled by our passion to share what we have learned from all of our clients over the past two years. They are the true heroes who trusted us enough to share a glimpse into their worlds. We are inspired by you, protective of you, and are also proud to work alongside and with you.

To Dr. Bruce Perry and Oprah Winfrey, thank you for writing your book *What Happened To You*. It re-ignited a spark by providing the neuroscience and stories to validate what we knew to be true through our experiences both inside and outside of our offices. And to the author, Charlie Mackesy, of *The Boy, The Mole, The Fox and The Horse,* who reminds us that we really don't know what's on the inside unless we share it with others.

To David Gentile, who believed in us from the beginning and continues to be one of our biggest supporters. The emotional contagion of his giving heart spurred our motivation to pursue this series of books. His artwork beautifully illustrates the essences of our words. He is a true philanthropist and family man, full of generational wisdom and creativity. Thank you for your forever friendship and your giving heart.

To Lisa Hoffman, who took a chance on us and gave us confidence when we needed it most. Lisa is a steadfast, insightful, and talented woman, who is a phenomenal publicist, editor, and now a forever friend.

To our publishers, Marianne Kilroy and Suzanne Donnelly, who saw our vision and helped make it a reality. They didn't waste a single minute. They helped us refuel when we were out of gas. We love the personal touch and working local.

To Carron's aunt, Lisa Eby, for her wisdom and willingness to wade through early streams of writing and fine tune later edits. When we couldn't find the right words, she helped us find them. She is an example of generational wisdom and the power of coming together! As an experienced life coach, she knows people. She understands the importance of mental health and finding ways to pursue your passion.

To Miranda Lucas, our genuine and talented graphic designer. You are a hidden gem with soothing energy and a true gift for seeing the big picture. You create beauty and flow with layouts and graphics. Thank you for putting up with our disorganized, tangential drafts as we found our creative voices.

To Corie English, our photographer who took amazing photos capturing the essence of what we wanted to convey. She inspired us with her bright personality and unwavering support.

To Sarah Golder, a freelance photographer and student at American University in Washington D.C. Sarah is wise beyond her years and was always one text away from creating the engaging graphics all while navigating her freshman year, out of state, amidst the pandemic.

To Dr. Van Horn and KC Psych Pros, who are great collaborators and provide invaluable resources to the community, including groups and IOP services. To Dr. Julie Brown, a fabulous pediatrician, friend, and collaborator who values mental health as much as we do. To Village Pediatrics, who welcomed Dr. Danda into their work family, support all her endeavors, and consistently share their wisdom. These are great examples of community partnerships.

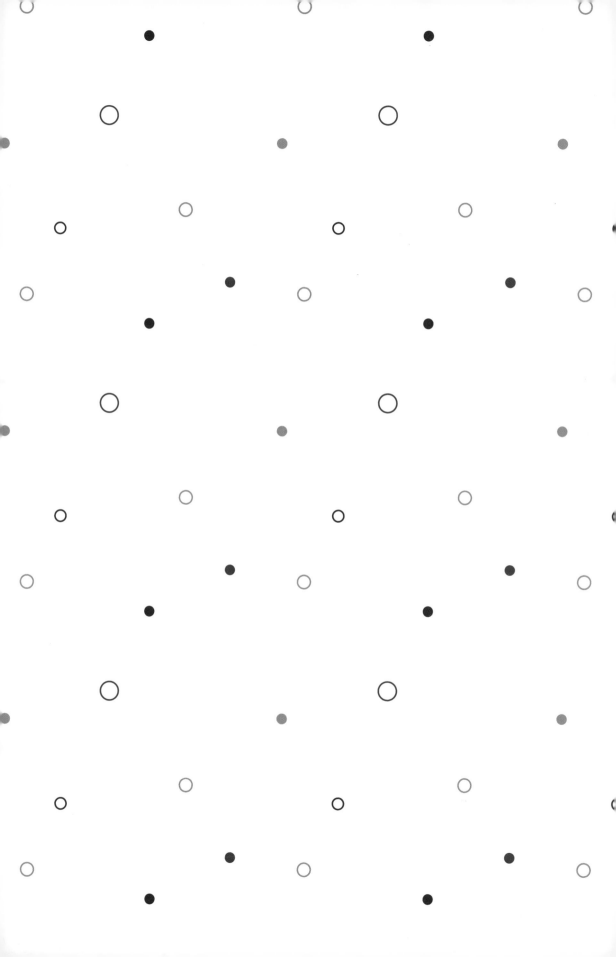